A MOUSE
IN THE HOUSE

by Michèle Dufresne • Illustrated by Sterling Lamet

Pioneer Valley Educational Press, Inc.

"A mouse!" cried Mom.
"A mouse! There's a mouse
in the house!"

"Jasper," said Mom.
"Go and catch the mouse.
It's your job to catch
the mouse!"

Jasper looked at the mouse.
It ran up and down in the kitchen.
It ran in and out of a little hole.

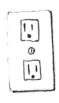

Jasper yawned and went to sleep.
Tomorrow he would catch
the mouse.

"A mouse!" cried Katie.
"A mouse!
There's a mouse in the house!"
"Jasper," said Katie.
"Go and catch the mouse.
It's your job
to catch the mouse!"

6

Jasper looked at the mouse.
It ran up and down
in Katie's room.
It ran in and out
of a little hole.
Jasper yawned
and went to sleep.
Tomorrow he would catch
the mouse.

"A mouse!" cried Mom.

"A mouse!" cried Katie. "A mouse! There's a mouse in the house!"

"Jasper," they said. "Go and catch the mouse. It's your job to catch the mouse!"

Jasper looked at the mouse.
It ran up and down
in the living room.
It ran in and out
of a little hole.
Jasper yawned
and went to sleep.
Tomorrow he would catch
the mouse.

"Oh, look," said Katie.
"The mouse is eating
Jasper's tuna fish."

Jasper woke up and looked
at the mouse.
It **was** eating his tuna fish!
Jasper jumped up and ran
after the mouse.

Now there's no mouse
in the house.